To the Cottrell Family
with best wishes from
John Prescott

Crowthorne

in old picture postcards volume 2

by
Martin Prescott

European Library - Zaltbommel/Netherlands MCMLXXXVII

GB   ISBN 90 288 3422 2 / CIP

© 1987 European Library - Zaltbommel/Netherlands

European Library in Zaltbommel/Netherlands publishes among other things the following series:

IN OLD PICTURE POSTCARDS *is a series of books which sets out to show what a particular place looked like and what life was like in Victorian and Edwardian times. A book about virtually every town in the United Kingdom is to be published in this series. By the end of this year about 300 different volumes will have appeared. 1,500 books have already been published devoted to the Netherlands with the title* **In oude ansichten.** *In Germany, Austria and Switzerland 650, 100 and 25 books have been published as* **In alten Ansichten;** *in France by the name* **En cartes postales anciennes** *and in Belgium as* **In oude prentkaarten** *and/or* **En cartes postales anciennes** *150 respectively 400 volumes have been published.*

For further particulars about published or forthcoming books, apply to your bookseller or direct to the publisher.

This edition has been printed and bound by Grafisch Bedrijf De Steigerpoort in Zaltbommel/Netherlands.

INTRODUCTION

This is the second volume of 'Crowthorne in old picture postcards'. The first has been surprisingly successful: two editions are now sold out. Yet Crowthorne is one of the least well-known of all sizeable villages: there is now a population of about 10 000 who consider themselves inhabitants. Another surprising thing is how many old photographs have surfaced, few of them actual postcards, to provide the 108 pictures for this volume.

The village of Crowthorne was essentially Victorian in origin. Before Wellington College (1859) and Broadmoor Asylum (1863) were opened, Crowthorne was only an old forest place name for the junction point of the Bigshot, Easthampstead and Sandhurst deer-walks in the Royal Forest of Windsor. Strictly speaking the only dwelling then existing in what is now the parish of Crowthorne, was the White Cottage (plate 32) near Brooker's Corner, the site of the original 'Crow Thorn' shown in miniature on Norden's 1607 Survey of Windsor Forest. Edgbarrow Cottage (plate 54) and Windy Ridge (plate 102) lie in other parishes.

WELLINGTON. The College is unique among public schools in being both a national memorial, and a royal foundation. The great Duke of Wellington died in 1852. It was generally agreed that he should be commemorated by the erection of a national monument. The second Duke proposed that a bronze statue of his father should stand in 'every considerable town' in England. Fortunately this project was not accepted: instead the Queen and Prince Albert approved the plan put forward by the Prime Minister, Lord Derby, to set up a charitable institution in the form of a school to educate the orphaned children of army officers. The money was to be raised by public subscription, and later a day's pay was required from every officer and soldier of the British Army. The appeal went well, and in 1853 the Queen granted the College a Charter of Incorporation.

Various sites were suggested, including Kneller Hall at Twickenham and Chelsea Hospital. But eventually the Sandhurst site was chosen, for a number of reasons, such as the abundance of building materials in the area, especially local building bricks; the fact that the Reigate to Reading railway ran close by; but primarily because the land was cheap. Mr. Gibson of Sandhurst Lodge offered 12 acres free, and another 120 more at £10 an acre. The architect was to be John Shaw. As we shall see, Queen Victoria laid the foundation stone in 1856. E.W. Benson, the first master (vol 1. plate 2) was only appointed in 1858. The original 76 pupils arrived on 20th January 1859, nine days before the official opening by the Queen.

BROADMOOR. The 'Criminal Lunatic Asylum' opened its doors on 27th May 1863; but its origin may be traced back to the case of James Hadfield, who in 1800 tried to assassinate George III at Drury Lane. He was prima facie guilty of high treason; but was obviously quite mad. Confinement neither in prison nor in Bethlem Hospital (Bedlam) for the insane, was appropriate. So the Criminal Lunatic Act 1800 was passed, under which Hadfield and those like him could be detained 'until his Majesty's Pleasure be known'.

Only in 1856 was it decided to build a state asylum, and Broadmoor was constructed on the plans of Sir Joshua Jebb, architect of Pentonville prison. The question is often asked: 'Why here?' But the answer seems obvious: the area round Bagshot Heath was one of the least populated parts of the Home Counties. Broadmoor remained a criminal lunatic asylum until 1948, long after it was realised that 'criminal lunatic' and 'guilty but insane' were contradictions in terms. In that year 'criminal lunatics' became 'Broadmoor Patients', furthermore Broadmoor itself was renamed 'Broadmoor Institution'. Finally in 1960 the name was changed to 'Broadmoor Hospital', and that of former warders/attendants to Broadmoor Nurses.

It must be obvious that from the beginning Crowthorne was constructed to service Wellington and Broadmoor; and so it continued for many years. But as the 20th century wore on, the area became part of the 'dormitory belt' of the metropolis. Also a number of research establishments moved into the district, like the Meteorological Office to Bracknell. Between 1958 and 1963 the (Transport and) Road Research Laboratory was set up just north of the village. Now the Thames Valley, sometimes known as the 'Western Corridor', is where the latest high technology and nuclear research are to be found. This has meant that the population of Berkshire is one of the fastest growing in the country.

The lay-out of this volume is in principle the same as that of volume 1: first Wellington, then Broadmoor and finally a 'conducted tour'. This last, however, is much wider in its scope than the previous one. In fact 33 of the pictures are of places outside the parish of Crowthorne; though almost every one is in a next-door parish. And the inhabitants of many of these places consider themselves residents of Crowthorne.

Lastly, the compiler would like to thank all the kind people who have lent him their pictures. In particular he wishes to express his gratitude to Dr. David Newsome, Master of Wellington, for so kindly permitting the use of College archive material, especially the 17 plates from Dr. Kempthorne's magnificent photograph album. Of course the College's copyright to all the pictures will be respected. There are too many other good friends who have given unstinted help to name them.

Once again the author wishes to express sincere thanks to his good friend David Withers for his marvellous photographic art work. Nothing has been too much trouble. Finally, as regards the written information about the various pictures, it has been necessary, as before, to seek information by word of mouth. Again Eddie Hallett and Ted Noakes have helped enormously, especially the latter with his knowledge of the Crowthorne Home Guard, otherwise 'Ted's Army'.

1. In about 1975 the Broadmoor estate staff, now extinct, were using a mechanical digger to open a trench on the south side of Lower Broadmoor Road for an electric cable, when it unearthed this massive stone. Mr. Cousins moved it over the road and incorporated it in his rockery at No. 5. It stands 82 cm. high, is 120 cm. in girth and weights some 300 kilos. The remarkable thing about it is its uniform mitre shape. Although basalt takes octagonal shapes (e.g. Giant's Causeway), few other rocks are regular in form.

2. All the foregoing suggested that this stone is indeed an artefact, in which case the exciting possibility arose that it is a paleolithic 'graven image', especially as a human face can be descried on the plate above. A distinguished geologist first confirmed that it is of sarsen, like the 'grey wethers' of Wiltshire; but then opined that it is a natural object, hitherto untouched by human hand. This was confirmed by the British Museum. It seems that a large bank of Bagshot (Surrey Green) sand tends to develop a core of sarsen by chemical action. This was a disappointment; but archeology is like that. (Mr. John Cousins of Broadmoor: photos D. Withers.)

3. As before we start with Wellington College. This painting hangs in the lobby outside the Master's study. It shows the south face of the College as the architect, John Shaw, planned it in the early 1850s, the equivalent of an architect's drawing. Neither of the two wing structures was built, the infirmary on the left and the chapel on the right – in any case Benson insisted on a Gothic chapel. It would seem that the College was meant to face south; but soon the north face, with Great Gate, came to be accepted as the front: hence the local saying: 'The College faces back to front' (Tom Newman). Burn, the first architect chosen, was prophetic when he reported in 1854: 'The nature of the grounds and general aspect, and the public and other roadways appear to me to point out conclusively that the approach and entrance to the building should be on the north and north-east, and the principal front face toward the south and south-west...' (The Master of Wellington.)

4. The foundation stone of Wellington College was laid by Queen Victoria on 2nd June 1856. She was accompanied by the Prince Consort, their three sons and four daughters, together with a huge crowd. In this picture the Royal Family are gathered round the foundation stone, 'which squatted importantly beneath an impressive, if garish, awning, which was balanced on four slender highly coloured poles. The awning dominated all – a luxurious thing, fat, solid and plush; looking for all the world like an outsize Victorian Hat' (Dr. Newsome). After the ceremony there was a splendid military review of nearly 12 000 troops, many recently returned from the Crimea. The Queen officially opened the College at a 'short and somewhat private' ceremony on 29th January 1859, nine days after the arrival of the first 76 pupils. (Wellington Archive.)

5. Here is another impression of the stone-laying ceremony. As the print is so small in this reproduction, the names of the Royals are given in legible form left to right: Regent of Baden; Prince Albert; D. of Cambridge; Pr. Mary of Cambridge; Pr. Fr. William of Prussia; Prince Alfred; Princess Helena; Pr. Louisa; Pr. Arthur; The Queen; Pr. Royal; Pr. of Wales. The Queen was in white; the Prince Consort in the full uniform of a Field Marshal. The three royal princes, all in highland dress, were Albert Edward, Prince of Wales, later Edward VII; Alfred (Affie), later Duke of Edinburgh, after whom, not King Alfred, the local pub was named; Arthur (Duke of Connaught). The second eldest princess married Prince Christian of Denmark (see vol. I, plate 10). The Prussian prince became the first German emperor. (Wellington Archive.)

6. This grim photograph of the College from the south-west must have been taken soon after the opening from the point of view where the infirmary had been planned. The heath around was still as blasted as could be; though it would appear that a number of shrubs had been established close against the south front. It is not known who were the figures on the balcony and at ground level. (Wellington Archive.)

7. The nave of Wellington College Chapel was completed four years after the opening. This Gothic structure, architected by Gilbert Scott, was primarily inspired by Benson and Prince Albert, despite their conflicting views on its design. The Prince laid the foundation stone in 1861, only months before his death from typhoid. It was consecrated by Bishop Wilberforce of Oxford two years later, and this photograph shows it in the same year, 1863. It is reported that when the Queen visited Wellington in 1864, she was shown the foundation stone laid by her darling Albert, and was so overcome with grief that she witdrew in tears. Maybe that was why she did not revisit the College for 36 years (see plate 14).

8. This photograph and its companion opposite were taken in 1869 from a viewpoint to the north of College, here looking across that part of the lake which was later to be made into the swimming pool. The Firs was owned latterly by a branch of the Lushington family, who kept a stable of horses. It survived till comparatively recent times: it appears on the 1939 Ordnance Survey map, and seems to have been demolished shortly after 1945 and replaced by three bungalows. Heatherly was renamed the Talbot. It has been much altered and added to. (Wellington Archive.)

9. This view was somewhat further east than the previous one. In the left foreground lay the well-known White Bridge. The Towers was the preparatory school set up by Dr. Spurling in 1867 (see plates 75 and 76). Heatherside was best known as a convalescent military hospital during the First World War. It was later renamed Greystoke as a College master's house, and was demolished in the 1970s. (Wellington Archive.)

The east end c.1870

Douro House   East Lodge   Carr's   St.Patricks   LaurelCottage   Edgbarrow
(Wellesley)   (Upcott)   (Douro)   (The Cottage)   Lodge

10. Here we have the back of the houses lining the Sandhurst Road at the east end of College in about 1870. To help with orientation it may be noted that the location of the eastern approach to the kilometre was, and is between East Lodge and Carr's (Upcott). The Mordaunt Gate has now been moved some way down the Kilometre: the houses are still there; but with all the building going on, their future must be somewhat problematical. (Wellington Archive.)

11. This Master's Lodge was built in 1865. Hitherto the Master had been accommodated in an apartment over Great Gate. Successive Masters lived here until 1940, when the Lodge suffered severe damage by enemy action, and had to be demolished (see plate 19). A new Lodge of somewhat more modest proportions was built here after the war and completed in 1953. (Kempthorne Album.)

12. The Rev. E.C. Wickham became the second Master of Wellington when he succeeded Benson in 1873. There is no 'Head Master'. By a remarkable coincidence he was first educated at Eagle House Preparatory School in Hammersmith, where his father was head master, but that was a quarter of a century before he came to Wellington, and another 13 years before Eagle House moved to Little Sandhurst. Wickham seems to have been a less dynamic character than Benson, and only rose to be Dean of Lincoln, whereas Benson went on to become Archbishop of Canterbury. (Wellington Archive.)

13. This seems a very ordinary picture of a steam train running between Blackwater and Wellington College stations. What does make it interesting is the hand-written caption that Kempthorne had subscribed: 'At 30 miles an hour. Exposure 1/50 second.' It must have been comparatively lately that fast film had made it possible to take photographs of moving objects without time exposures. (Kempthorne Album.)

14. Here is The Queen's delayed visit to Wellinton on Mafeking Day, 19th May 1900 (a sheer coincidence, of course). What is so extraordinary about this photograph, taken from Great Gate looking down to the lakes, was that the Queen's victoria (?) was occupied only by herself and her ladies-in-waiting: there were no footmen up behind. The coachman was hatless and in 'scruff ordner' with a tarpaulin apron as worn by brewers' draymen. No doubt the 'Widow of Windsor' was not concerned about such things; but she must had have equerries... She was dead eight months later. (Wellington Archives.)

15. Here is another royal occasion: King Edward VII is standing centre left talking, one supposes to Randall Davidson, Archbishop of Canterbury; while the third Master, the Rev. Dr. Bertram Pollock, stands on the far left of the picture. Pollock made a great point of cultivating the royal visitor as well as other dignitaries. The King visited the College in 1904, 1907 and 1909. It seems most likely that this was the last occasion, the Jubilee Speech Day to celebrate the half century. Probably this photograph shows the two variegated conifers being planted, as remembered by George Daniel.

16. It may be safely assumed that this is King Edward VII being driven down Crowthorne High Street on the way to Wellington College; and in view of the throng that had turned out, it must have been a very special occasion. That would suggest that this was the 1909 Jubilee. The photograph was taken from the chemist shop opposite the Iron Duke, as were all the others. Today the building has been replaced by New Pharmacy Court.

Motor Landaulet presented to the late Headmaster of Wellington College by Wellingtonians and others interested in the School, on his elevation to the See of Norwich.

17. At the end of the 1910 Lent term Dr. Pollock left Wellington to be made Bishop of Norwich. It was decided by Old Wellingtonians and others that the See of Norwich was so large that the Bishop would need some improved form of transport, so they clubbed together and bought him this 15 h.p. 'Landaulet'. As will be observed, it was supplied by Vincents of Reading, a firm that still exists. Unfortunately there are no records extant of the vehicle; but the Motor Museum at Beaulieu confirms that it was a Daimler. (Wellington Archive.)

18. The 4th Master, W.W. Vaughan, the first non-clerical head, governed the College from 1910 to 1921. It was not an easy time, including as it did the First World War and the subsequent Spanish Flu epidemic in 1919. Then on Sunday 9th March 1919 fire broke out in the Orange Dormitory, once used as the chapel, and destroyed it utterly. Fortunately there were no casualties apart from the Bursar's dislocated thumb. In his book 'A Victorian School' Tallboys wrote: 'In such events there is often an incident of comic relief; and I shall always remember the appearance of a primitive little fire engine, I think it was from Binfield, breasting its way up the drive and drawn by two cart horses, their harness consisting mostly of rope, and the hose, when brought into effect, scarcely reaching to the Anglesey windows.' (Wellington Archive.)

19. Wellington was to experience a much worse tragedy. On 8th October 1940 the Master, R.P. Longden, was killed by enemy action. What happened was best described in the words of the present Master, David Newsome: 'The alert had sounded at 7.30 that night. The boys had taken to the shelters and the Master had visited A.R.P. Headquarters. He had then returned to the Lodge for his dinner. Soon after 8 p.m. a bomb dropped nearby and Longden went to the door of the Lodge to see if any damage had been done. At that moment a high-explosive bomb fell in the forecourt of the Lodge. The Master was killed instantly, the heavy porch collapsing on top of him. No one else was hurt.' It is reported that his car ended up in a tree. (Wellington Archive.)

20. This was the well-known 'White-Bridge' when it was still made of timber; it has now been replaced by a concrete structure. It used to lead from College through the woods to Duke's Ride; but that access is now closed. The scene is usually photographed from the east; but here it is from the west with two Wellingtonians in the background.

21. Here is the approach from Wellington College to Ambarrow bridge. It reminds Ted Noakes of a terrifying experience he had as a small boy. His father was a butcher and Ted used to accompany the van-man on his rounds. One day they went down to Sandhurst and the driver tied the horse to a railing near St. Michael's Church, and left Ted in charge. Something frightened the animal, which broke its tether and bolted with poor young Ted along the road to Crowthorne station. It veered over this bridge, galloped through the College estate to Edgbarrow Star on the Sandhurst Road and turned left along the High Street. Mr. Lightfoot managed to slow it down a little, and Ted jumped out awkwardly and broke a bone in his foot. The runaway was eventually halted at Easthampstead.

22. Now we turn to 'Broadmoor Criminal Lunatic Asylum' opened on 27th May 1863, four years after Wellington College. Here is the Main Gate, built by Sir Joshua Jebb in his Pentonville style. It has not changed much since then, apart from two new entrances on the left for staff and visitors; and is one of the parts of the Victorian building which will survive the current 're-build' (1986). It is to become a museum of the history of Broadmoor. However, it will be masked by the new buildings and will be invisible from this angle.

23. These nine elegant ladies in their sombre bombazine (?) were the female staff of Broadmoor Asylum in 1896. She on the left of the back row was Ellen Tyman, mother of Mrs. Ena Pearce of Pinehill Road; her sister Gertrude, mother of Mrs. Muriel Gale of Grant Road, was second from the right in the front row. They all had to be unmarried, and remained so till the Second World War, when because of staff shortages the wives of attendants who had gone to the war were allowed to join the staff. Until the 1950s all the staff, male and female, had rooms and slept on the wards. (Mrs. E. Pearce.)

24. This photograph is from the Kempthorne album, and so dates from about 1890. It shows Broadmoor chapel from the north-east. The shrubbery is now the location of the central court-yard with the Main Gate just off the picture to the right. This is the less familiar view of the chapel, since it is now obscured by more modern buildings. Of course it will also escape the 'rebuild'. (Kempthorne Album.)

25. This picture, also from the camera of Dr. Kempthorne, is contemporary with that opposite. It shows the old Superintendent's garden backed by what is now Essex House. The lumps of masonry on the lawn were probably Bath stone left over from building operations. Since then they have been used to form the grotto on what is now known among the patients as 'Watership Down'. The grotto is sadly overgrown. (Kempthorne Album.)

BROADMOOR ASYLUM, CROWTHORNE.

26. Here we have the Hospital Terrace from the west. It is not seen by members of the general public, unless they have a 'Terrace Visit' with a patient. The buildings are, from the left, Dorset House, the Superintendent's office, chapel, Kent House and Essex House. It seems that all these, together with the gatehouse, will survive the 'rebuild'. In fact the terrace front will be the only part of old Broadmoor that will be visible from outside, to the south.

27. York House, part of the female wing, is facing us here, with Lancaster House off the picture on the right. The bandstand is still there; but has been glassed in. It is understood that all this will go in the 'rebuild'. The bowling green and croquet lawn are in the foreground.

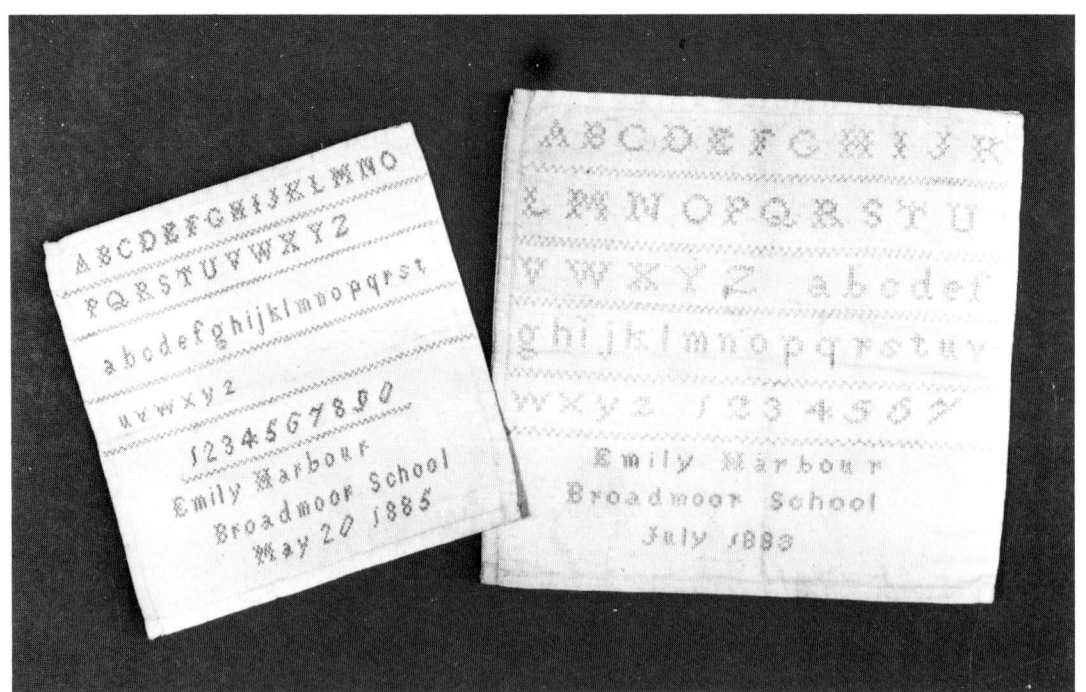

28. We now turn to Broadmoor School, used by the children of the staff. Over a hundred years ago a little girl called Emily Harbour did these pieces of embroidery. When she grew up, she married a Mr. Ifould, the proprietor of the Waterloo Hotel, and they began the family business for four generations of Ifoulds. The hotel has now passed into other hands, and Michael, the last of the line, lives in the West Country. These pieces of embroidery are what are generally understood to be 'samplers'; but...

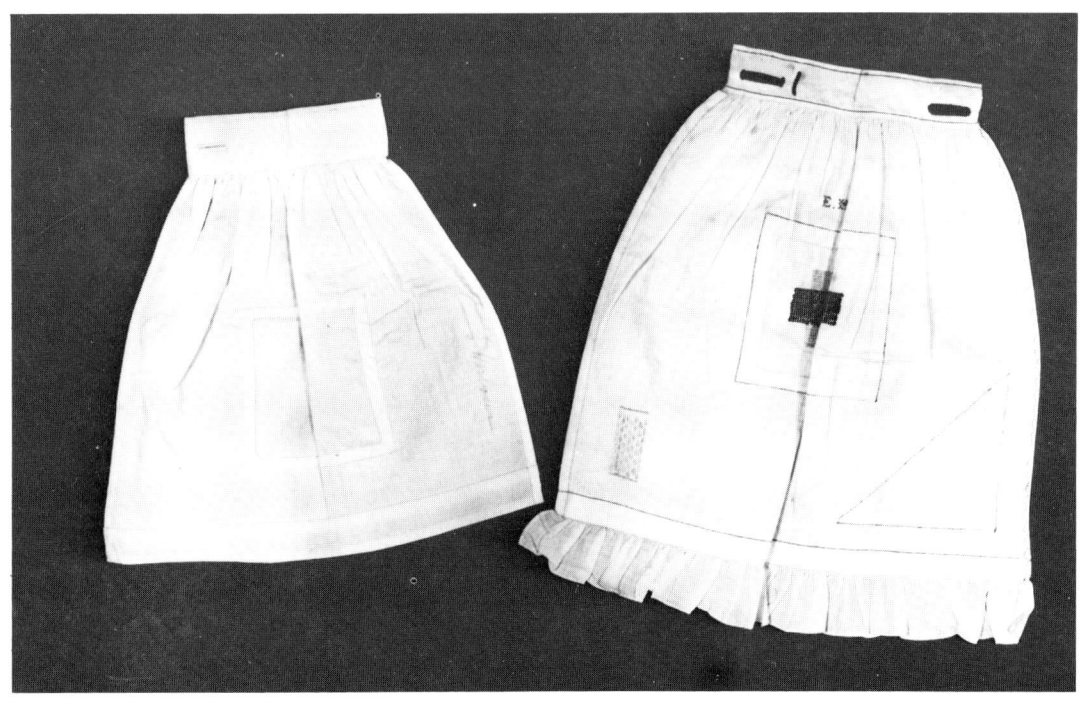

29. ... these must surely be the true samplers, that is cotton material, in this case doll's aprons, embroidered with every stitch in the book – buttonholes, eyes for hooks, patches, hem-stitching, etc. It must be remembered that little Emily did all this without modern artificial light. Would anyone be capable of this kind of work today? These masterpieces are the treasured heirlooms of Emily's grandson... (Chris Brady.)

30. Broadmoor Sports Day, like other similar events, was a very important occasion in days gone by. Here the Broadmoor Elementary School maypole team of 1924 stands grouped on the cricket field. Their names from left to right, back to front are: Lucy Gordon, Edith Bennet, Bill Unwin, Dorothy Cordery, Olive Groves, Margery Freeman, George Holdaway and Harold Hale.
Jack Lawrence, Betty Taylor, Jack Cottrell, Bill Hitchcock, Joan Justice, Flossie Nunn, John Gibbons, Betty Lawrence and John Holdaway.
Eileen Owen, Gilbert Gordon, George Cater, Gladys Watts, Alec Cottrell, Peggy Taylor, George Watts, Ethel Nunn and John Nunn.

31. There were two Terraces at Broadmoor: one inside the walls (see plates 26 and 27), the other outside (here). It appears that these were the first outside houses built on this site: they are said to have been used by the workmen building the Asylum. There is even a story that they were designed by Prince Albert; but this seems unlikely. Anyway, they were all demolished in 1985. Fortunately Mick Goswell had the sense to photograph them as the roofs were being stripped. (Mick Goswell.)

32. Now we embark on a conducted tour of the village starting at the location where it all began. White Cottage is one of the two original buildings of what became Crowthorne. It was a forester's cottage close by the site of the Crow Thorn, or as it is now known, Brooker's Corner. Mr. Mitchell, the present owner, was told, when he arrived that it used to be known as 'Widow Brooker's Cottage': it would seem that the eponymous Mr. Brooker must have been a forester. The building dates from before 1834; but has been much extended. This view shows most clearly what must have been its original form with central chimney. (Photo David Withers.)

33. This is the earliest picture to hand of the Lightfoot family, with four generations in their garage business. This photograph of Roy Lightfoot dates from about 1905, as David says his father was born in 1904. It shows Roy sitting on a horse with his little legs sticking out and supported by his mother. Roy was the second generation, as his father Ernest started the garage, originally a wheelwrights. The business has passed from father to son: Ernest to Roy to David, and eventually to Graham. (David Lightfoot.)

34. This motor car was the first that Ernest Lightfoot, of Ernest Lightfoot and Son, brought into the village: Mr. Lovick was earlier. David dates the picture about 1923. The car was built by a French firm: Sizarre et Naudin. Mr. and Mrs. Lightfoot are seated therein. As the two-seater was French, it had left hand drive: it would seem Mrs. L. was in the driver's seat, which must have been a little unusual at the time. (David Lightfoot.)

35. This picture shows a function organised by the Berkshire Bee Keepers Association. The date is not known; but the location is: a then vacant triangle of land on the south side of Brooker's Corner (then Broadmoor Road), and now enclosing 'Apple Trees'. The house opposite is Hope Cottage, with Ruscombe Cottages on the right and Havelock Cottages on the left. Canon Coleridge stands firmly in the centre, with Teddy Stokes next to him holding the bee-skip. Gertie Stokes calls attention to the fact that her father's left eye had been closed by a bee-sting. (Miss G. Stokes.)

Broadmoor Road — Crowthorne

36. The name of this road has now been changed to Upper Broadmoor Road but all the houses are still there. The building nearest the camera on the left, Oak Cottages (nos. 29-31) were acquired shortly before the First World War by Mr. William Pearmain, who set up a small workshop there to repair mechanical items. He soon began to attend to motor cars. So began the family garage business of W. Pearmain and Sons, which of course is still in business on the High Street. What was not yet in existence in this picture was the Broadmoor estate generally known as the White City.

37. Here is a photograph of Miss Louisa Goddard in old age at the door of her house, Melita, in Wellington Road. Her importance in the village was as key figure at the Crowthorne C. of E. School in Dukes Ride for many, many years. She entered the school as a 5 year old infant in 1876; became a monitor in 1886 and an adult teacher three years later. She retired as virtual deputy head in 1932 after 56 years in all. She died in February 1965 at Pinewood Hospital. Known to her pupils variously as Louie or Judy, she was a real martinet; but greatly loved. Any former pupil returning to Crowthorne always went to see her.

38./39. It has proved extraordinarily difficult to identify these members of the Crowthorne Home Guard, despite exhaustive enquiries among the decreasing number of survivors from 1944, and in the local press. What one wishes to avoid is an irate lady saying: 'You have put 'unknown', but everyone knew my Jimmy!' Anyway, here goes E & O E: W. Searly, H. St. George, R. Burtwell, W. Ward, R. Castle, F. Smith, C. Passmore, unknown, unknown, E. Watts, J. Mason, J. Samuels, C. Milam and J. Edwards.
W. Gear, C. Cripps, unknown, unknown, G. Austin, J. Saunders, J. Edwards, E. Maugham, J, Sheffield, unknown, unknown, F. White, D. Dean and D. Greenaway.
Unknown, W. Grinstead, C. Burtwell, H. Williams, J. Spear, F. Thomas, E. Mason, unknown, unknown,

unknown, unknown, J. Justice, W. Brown, unknown and K. Pratt.
G. Donnelly, G. Burtwell, R. Sandy, J. Condick, W. Hands, F. Ashby, R. Herridge, J. Perry, unknown, J. Fern, D. Clarke, E. Noakes and W. Girling.
A. Fullbrook, G. Palmer, H. Woods, A. Blunden, J. Lindop, W. Watts, unknown, E. Lloyd, F. Brasher and A. Butcher.
65 members of the Crowthorne platoon Home Guard grouped in front of their headquarters, the C. of E. School. There were also platoons at Broadmoor and Wellington College. The Battalion H.Q. was at Pinefields, now a clothing factory.

40. The caption to this picture reads: 'Surrey Villas.' It took quite a lot of searching to establish that the building consists of numbers 30 and 32 Dukes Ride. The Church of England School would have been just off the picture to the left. Number 32 has been a dentist's surgery for many years. (Kempthorne Album.)

41. On the back of this postcard is written: '1919. Celebration Day for peace. Crowthorne.' The locale was the 'village green' opposite the Prince Alfred, where the police station now stands. The occasion was Armistice Day 1919, 11 a.m. 11th November, the hour and day that Armistice had been signed the year before. Lutyens' Cenotaph was unveiled on Armistice Day 1920. Thereafter the 'two minute silence' was instituted, presumably because a parade would disrupt a working day. During the Second World War the silence was abandoned, so as not to interrupt war production. After 1945 we had the dead of two world wars to commemorate, and Remembrance Sunday was introduced for the Sunday nearest 11th November.

42. We turn into the north end of the High Street in the days of the horse and cart. The three shops shown were: Stokes on the right (now the Midland Bank), Harveys on the left (now Woodage/Londis) and Ives – later Tames (now Lloyds Bank). It will be noticed that the Prince Alfred's front has recently (1985) been refurbished much as it was then. The debris in the middle of the road reminds a surprising number of people how we used to collect it with bucket and shovel to spread on our roses or rhubarb – or sell at one old penny a bucket: hence the local cry: 'Coo-ee! Coming dunging? Bring your own shovel.' Few people, however, recall that in London anyway small boys used to collect dog droppings for use in the tannery business to make Morocco leather. It seems there was an exceedingly vulgar jingle current: 'Dirty Dickie Diver, dog shit finder.'

43. Here is Stokes' shop, remembered with affection by old residents as the supplier of sweets, cigarettes and many other sorts of things: in fact a real village shop. The business was started by John Stokes, younger brother of Teddy S., in the shop now known as the 'Flower Basket'. After his death his widow, Elizabeth, transferred it to the site shown above, which is why it was called 'E. Stokes'. This picture shows (left to right) Edie Spicer (apprentice), Cissie Stokes and Elsie Stokes. It is generally agreed that the occasion was Victory in Europe Day (6th May 1945) in view of the red, white and blue ribbons in the window. (Gertie Stokes.)

44. This old picture has proved something of a puzzle. It was said to be No. 10 Forest Road, the earliest house built there, and now belonging to Nurse Gurden; but inspection immediately proved otherwise. The conformation of the building with two bays unseparated by a door downstairs and two single windows upstairs is somewhat unusual. A complete survey of the village revealed only one house of that design, No. 22 Cambridge Road. So that must be the one, unless you know otherwise, dear reader!

45. This was the old Baptist Church in about 1949. The building was originally bought from Calcot for £100 in 1918, and transported to Crowthorne in sections. In August it was reported that 'Mr. Wheatley and Mr. Johnson with their men, engines and trollies have performed the feat, and now the work of rebuilding is in hand'. 30 years later the board shows that the preacher at morning service was Sister Bessie Sellwood (appointed Deaconess in charge autumn 1949); at the evening service 'Mr. G.R. ****'. This must have been George Bell (on the right), who was in charge of this Sunday School, assisted by Mr. and Mrs. T. Bowles. Among the children the following have been identified (in alphabetical order): Mick Bell, Maurice and Marina Cox, Ben, Peter and Ann Gater, Maureen and Pat Rowe, Netta Taylor and Andrew Watts. The brick church dates from 1954. (Mick Bell.)

46. This shop is now the left hand half of the Berkshire Cycle Company premises. It then belonged for a number of years to the present Mrs. K. Ashby, the second of the six Donnelly girls: Nell, Kath, Dot, Nancy, Lilian and Ivy Kate. The Donnellys, as shown in volume I, were very much at the centre of things at the beginning of this century, running the bakery, the dairy and later a coal merchants. Kath married Mr. Ashby, the chimneysweep. She is still living near Bristol, where she celebrated her 90th birthday on 19th April 1986.

Sworder, Crowthorne, Berks.

47. This is still a greengrocer and fruiterer under another name; but to old Crowthorne residents it remains Sworders. The business started in 1890 when Walter Sworder rented a shop in Church Street. He married a daughter of William Spear, the builder, who built them this shop in 1896, with living accommodation over and a large cellar, originally a quarry. Next year Walter opened a horse and carriage business in the sheds on the left. When he gave up the shop, his son Sidney took over: he was married to Nancy, the fourth of the Donnelly girls. Nancy Sworder managed the business when her husband went off to the Second World War, and carried on until her death in 1970. (Joyce Simpson, née Sworder.)

48. We have now turned up Wellington Road. One of the things that strikes us about village life a century or so ago was how the villagers used to occupy and entertain themselves. Here we have a baby show on the football ground at the north west corner of the Morgan Recreation Ground. The lady in the centre of the front row was Mrs. Beauchamp; and the baby on her lap, which must have won the first prize, was Fred Beauchamp, who is still living at Rothwell House, aged 83. This would appear to date the photograph at about 1903 or 1904.

49. Here is a photograph of the Gymkhana Committee in front of 33 Wellington Road. In the centre of the front row is the inevitable Ted Stokes, who ran just about everthing in the village. Another interesting personality is the lady on the extreme left, who shall remain nameless, as she was the subject of THE village scandal, and her great-niece still lives in Crowthorne. She was known as 'Mrs. Tar and Feather' because she was tarred and feathered by the soldiery. That is fact; but the legend goes on that they were Canadian soldiers in the First World War, and that afterwards they took her into Camberley and dumped her on the island in the R.M. College, Sandhurst lake. That is fantasy. In fact the date was 1913, the soldiers were British, from a tented camp at Easthampstead Park (Territorials, presumably), and she was found in a ditch at Caesar's Camp.

50. The 1894 smithy is now in process of demolition, and was photographed in 1985 before its final disappearance. It was originally a Mr. Bartlett's forge, and was taken over by his nephew and apprentice G.R. Vaughan (see volume 1 plate 32). Much later it was acquired by Nigel Edwards as part of his iron-mongery and tinsmith business. The smithy has been derelict for a number of years; but the shop in front is occupied by the Wellington Vintners. (Photograph: David Withers.)

51. Broadmoor Avenue for some reason is now known as Lower Broadmoor Road. It has not changed much, except that it is broader, the trees are bigger and the railings have gone. What is interesting about the narrow strip of land between the Morgan Recreation Ground and Addiscombe Road is that in the 1816-17 Sandhurst Award connected with the Windsor Forest Inclosure Act (which ended the Royal Forest of Windsor) the strip was awarded to the proprietor of Sandhurst Lodge to give access from the Sandhurst Road to what is now the location of Broadmoor Hospital.

Crowthorne.

52. This is an old picture of the Iron Duke crossroads. From a comparison of the tree growths, it is earlier than that in volume 1 plate 39. In the left foreground can be distinguished the 'Bon Marche' haberdashery store, now another of the plethora of estate agents. Further on lay the chemist, probably Satchells, with the red lamp standing outside (now Old Pharmacy Court). On the right are the Iron Duke pub sign; the College houses; the end of the Iron Duke hall and the gardens in front of the Duke, with fencing and trees and all.

53. The traditional name for this tract of woodland was 'Cox's Woods', presumably from a previous owner. It lies some way down the Sandhurst Road on the left, near where there was a sawmill, at one time the property of Edward Jones, who later moved to Pinewood Avenue. Ted Noakes says that E. Jones felled many trees there; but this operation seems to have been twenty years or so earlier. (Kempthorne Album.)

54. Edgbarrow Cottage lies amidst these same 'Cox's Woods'. There seems little doubt that it was the earliest building in the vicinity; unless White Cottage (plate 32) is earlier, which seems unlikely. Edgbarrow Cottage was once a verderer's house, and so more important than a mere forester's; since a verderer was a judicial officer of the Royal Forest. It is clear that the entire front was that of the original building; but only one room in depth. The back of the house was added in 1945. The well, unlike the cottage, is a 'listed building'. (Photograph David Withers.)

55. The four windows at the front of the building are all identical, made of iron with leaded lights. This is the right hand downstair window. An acknowledged expert on the subject confirms that windows of this type were only constructed during the decade around 1750. So that dates the cottage very early indeed. There was a door between the two downstairs windows. Incidentally this seems to have been the 'Honeywoman's Cottage' mentioned by Dr. Newsome in his history of Wellington as a sort of precursor of 'Grubbies'. (Photograph David Withers.)

56. The history of Eagle House Preparatory School, now down the Sandhurst Road, is a very long and fascinating one. In 1820 a certain Mr. Joseph Railton, a teacher from Cumberland, acquired a property known as Eagle House at Brook Green, Hammersmith, in order to set up a school for the sons of gentlemen. The house, built towards the end of the previous century, was constructed of red brick, fronted by a low brick wall, at each end of which stood a prominent pillar supporting an eagle cast in solid lead. These can be seen quite clearly on the print above; though the painter Whichelo seems to have missed them when he attempted to paint the appearance of the original building. (Eagle House School.)

EAGLE HOUSE, WIMBLEDON HIGH STREET. BUILT 1613.

57. The second headmaster was the Reverend Edward Wickham, whose son, a scholar of the school, was to become the second Master of Wellington. The next head, the Reverend Edward Huntingford, moved the school to Wimbledon in 1860. It has always been supposed that he took one of the eagles with him; but this is manifestly a mistake. For one thing the wing aspect is wrong; but more obviously the Wimbledon bird is made of stone, not lead. In fact it looks as if the eagle was an integral part of the original building, which dates from 1613. It was already visited by Lord Nelson and Lady Hamilton shortly before Trafalgar in 1805. This could make Eagle House one of the oldest prep. schools in the land. (Eagle House School.)

58. At the end of the 1886 summer term the fourth headmaster, Dr. A.N. Malan, told the boys that there was exciting news on the notice board. This was that the school was to move forthwith to Sandhurst in Berkshire. Wimbledon was becoming too urbanised; but no one knows why he chose darkest Berkshire. It seems the building in Sandhurst had been constructed twenty years earlier by a Dr. Russell as a private residence – not as a lunatic asylum, as was the predictable school story. This sketch shows Eagle House in the 1880s. The school has celebrated its centenary at Sandhurst in 1986. (Eagle House School.)

59. In 1906 after 32 years Dr. Malan handed the school over to Mr. R. Bruce Lockhart, who for 21 years fashioned Eagle House in his own image. He and his family were all talented players of rugby football: one of his sons and two of his grandsons played for Scotland. Of the four heads during the years 1927 to 1968 Paul Wootton was the best remembered. In the latter years Eagle House was in effect taken over by Wellington College as its junior school. The picture above was taken in April 1984: it shows the second Eagle House still standing on Wimbledon High Street. The School has from time to time asked Wimbledon Corporation: 'Please can we have our eagle back,' but so far without success. (Eagle House School.)

60. We are now back in the centre of Crowthorne after our brief excursion into the parish of Sandhurst. Few people seem to know that this is Waterloo Place. The creeper-clad Iron Duke is on the far left. Next to it was a branch of the Wokingham butcher, W.T. Martin. (Incidentally Mr. Martin gave his money and his name to Martin's Pool). On the right lay the International Stores, which was still there after the Second World War; but the gas lighting (?) suggests that this picture dates from very much earlier.

61. Cooper's 'Reading, Crowthorne & District Carriers' operated widely; but mainly between Crowthorne and Reading. The office was in Church Street a greengrocers, now occupied by the Bradford & Bingley Building Society. The service carried people as well as goods. Twice a week on Tuesdays and Thursdays passengers could travel to Reading for 6 old pence return. It was a more convenient service than by train, which was somewhat intermittent and unreliable in those days.

Church Street, Crowthorne.

62. Probably the oldest part of the village, and certainly the earliest shops, are to be found on the north side of Church Street and the west side of High Street. Thus Ifould's Bakery, which is now G.M. News, was in 1866 used for 'Cottage Lectures' by the Reverend H.S.N. Lenny, Curate of Sandhurst, who eight years later became the first Vicar of Crowthorne. The end shop shown above was in recent years known as Douglas' Stores. It is sometimes said to have been a post office; but this seems unlikely, though there was a post box let into the wall. It is now Wesley's Wine Bar.

63. On the left of this rather dull picture of Church Road stand Nos. 39-41. Next door in the empty space was to be built No. 43, which became a police house occupied by one of our village 'bobbies'. Ted Noakes remembers Constable Porchmouth catching him and his brother Perce setting fire to the school woods, and giving them both a good hiding, as also did their father. There was another police house in Wellington Road, and at one time Crowthorne had a resident police sergeant and two constables. Now we have none. It is generally agreed that the best form of policing is the constable who lives on his beat; but there is no-one living in the police house next to the unmanned police station. It does seem a little crazy. To be fair there are reasons. Two are: decision making in the huge three county Thames Valley Police Authority are very centralised: furthermore policemen are now allowed to buy their own homes and not have to live in tied houses.

64. We now approach the churchyard of the Church of St. John Baptist, Crowthorne, from the south-east. This end of it was the first part to have graves dug. It then filled up over the years, with a 'New Churchyard' purchased in 1896. Now it is quite full. The gate shown was the entrance to the churchyard before the lychgate was constructed in 1913-14. (Mr. Peter Cracknell.)

65. This is a photograph of the lychgate taken some time between 1914 and 1921. It was on 21st February 1921 that it was dedicated as a village war memorial. (See volume 1 plate 53.) The names of the 105 men of Crowthorne who were killed in the First World War were inscribed on the four panels incorporated into the structure. Mercifully there are fewer on the 1935-1945 memorial close by: 23 men and 1 woman.

66. The first Vicar of Crowthorne, the Reverend H.S.N. Lenny, came up to the village from Sandhurst as Curate in 1866, then became Priest-in-Charge, and was made Vicar when a separate parish was formed in 1874. This picture of him with his choir must have been taken between 1874 and 1884 when he left for Cradley Heath in the Black Country. He died near Blackburn in 1912. Sadly nothing is known of the choir, all in Eton collars, and its choirmaster.

67. In 1985 a family of parishioners were on holiday in Totnes when they found this pencil sketch in a local shop. It shows Crowthorne Church in 1888, and was the work of General C. Dumbleton, Indian Army, late 10th Bengal Lancers. It appears that after his retirement he went to stay at Hawley, and used to tour the district with a sketchbook. Strangely it is the only known view of the church from before 1889, when the chancel was added. So no-one knows exactly what the east end looked like earlier, either externally or internally. Was there a window in the main arch? (The Bushnell family.)

68. This photograph of the chancel of the church being built was taken by Dr. Kempthorne at the end of the 1880s. One could have wished that he had turned his attention to the east end rather than to the Lady Chapel at the side. From the picture it might be thought that the memorial window to Maria Thomson had not yet been installed; but it is still invisible from this angle. The Chancel and Lady Chapel were dedicated in February 1889. (Kempthorne Album.)

69. This view of Crowthorne Church in the 1890s shows that the chancel together with the Lady Chapel and the north chapel had now been incorporated therein. It was taken by Dr. Kempthorne from the north-east, i.e. from the present location of Hobart. The north chapel was demolished in 1908 to make way for the new choir vestry. There is no picture extant showing what it was like inside. (Kempthorne Album.)

70. This photograph by Dr. Kempthorne of the Parish Church from the south-east must be contemporary with the previous one. Observation suggests that it must have been taken from the site of the present-day 'Queen's Rook', number 13 Waterloo Road. As always, the eye is struck by the quantity of self-sown trees around. There seems to be no trace of the big cedar. (Kempthorne Album.)

71. The west end of the church as it was nearly a century ago looks most strange to modern eyes. Like everywhere else in the village, it was smothered with trees, hedges and bushes. The peculiar apse was the baptistry containing the font, traditionally by the church door. However, it in fact tended to obstruct entry, especially to coffins; and in 1959 the font was moved to its present location. The apse was finally swallowed up in the St. Nicholas Hall and the Galilee Porch in 1968-69.

72. Here is an insoluble puzzle! This churchyard cross of Caldey stone must surely be a war memorial. It is not. It was set up in 1913-1914. Canon Coleridge wrote in the Parish Magazine: 'The Churchyard Cross (and lychgate) now being erected are respectively the gifts of two parishioners as 'Thank Offerings'. Round its base runs an inscription: *To the glory of God and in remembrance of many who without memorial rest in his loving keeping this cross is dedicated. A.D. 1913.*' A senior resident suggests it was for those who could not afford a headstone. Another says that the two anonymous benefactors were the Misses Blair.

73. Canon Coleridge celebrated his half century as Vicar of Crowthorne in 1944. The celebration seems to have been somewhat low key, and this group photograph is all the record that can be found of the occasion. Left to right: Mr. Goodband, headmaster of the Church School; Canon Groves, Rural Dean of Sonning; the Vicar; Bishop Parham of Oxford; and Miss Hunt and Mr. Croft, churchwardens. Canon Coleridge served another two years before retiring in 1946. He died aged 92 at St. John's Cottage, Church Street in 1949. The background to this picture is interesting; it is almost certainly the British Legion, which the Berkshire County Council used as a Rest Centre; but nobody seems to remember precisely what for.

74. Andrew Nugee succeeded Canon Coleridge as the fourth Vicar of Crowthorne in 1946. The patch over his right eye (?) catches our attention. This was a legacy of the Great War. At Hooge in July 1915 Temporary Lieutenant A.C. Nugee of the Rifle Brigade was horribly wounded by a 'whizz-bang' after only 18 days on the Western front: the two men next to him in the trench were killed outright: Andrew lost his right eye and his left was badly affected. Invalided out, he studied for the priesthood and was ordained in 1922. He learned to read the services in braille. He used to stump round the village, followed by his faithful dachshund, Tilly, recognizing his parishioners by the sound of their voices. He was greatly loved. In 1960 he moved to Broadwell on the border of Oxfordshire with Gloucestershire. (Parish Church.)

75. In 1867 Dr. Benson, the first Master of Wellington, authorised one of his senior assistant masters, the Reverend J.W. Spurling, to live out of College, and take junior boys as boarders and pupils. A piece of land was provided by the College, and 'Crowthorne Towers' preparatory school was built on the site of the present Towers Drive. This photograph by Dr. Kempthorne dated 1875 shows the school standing on the empty heathland. Clearly the Master expected that the Towers should be a junior school for Wellington; but Mr. Spurling was determined that his boys should go to whatever public school they wished. (Kempthorne Album.)

76. This is a later picture of Towers, though earlier than that in volume 1 plate 64. After the death of Mr. Spurling in 1899 there was a succession of headmasters, only four of whom are recorded by name: Mr. C.J.M. Wauton; a partnership of a Mr. Powell and Basil Carr, and the last head, Mr. N.M. Archdale. The school was demolished in 1938. All that survives of the entire complex is Pinefields, which was the school gymnasium, and is now a clothing factory. (See volume 1 plate 65.)

77. The Crowthorne Scouts figure at this stage of our conducted tour round the village, because the First Crowthorne Scout Troop was started by a Capt. Cautley in a hut in his garden at Barracane off Waterloo Road in 1909 or 1910. This photograph was taken between 1916 and 1919. Eddy Hallett, the small boy on the right of the back row, says that it was the Roll of Honour that stands in front of the group. The scoutmaster was John Crease, assisted by 'Jock' Brown.

78. The 1st Crowthorne Scouts are shown at their camp at Ringwood in August 1937. Their names were as follows, left to right, back row: Peter Tyler, Bill Robertson, Bert Lovick, Leonard Leakey ('Drip'), S.M., Jim Jaycock, Charlie Burnham and Don Waite. Front row: Reg Bullbeck, Alan Broadhead, Tony McGowran, Vic Cudlipp and Eddie North. Though only fifty years old, this picture is already something of a museum piece, especially to youngsters. The old scout hat and shorts must seem positively archaic. It appears that modern boys are sensitive about showing their knees, unlike their elders. (Bill Robertson.)

79. Father Daniel Boyle was parish priest to the Roman Catholic Church of the Holy Ghost in the New Wokingham Road for 25 years from 1948 to 1973. His was a late vocation, having had a full life in teaching and business before being ordained: a most reliable former parishioner was told that he also married and had two children; and that his entire family was killed in a car crash; though it has not been possible to confirm this. He came to Crowthorne at the age of fifty. His great achievement was to replace the old 'tin tabernacle' with the existing brick church opened in 1962. But he will be remembered much more for his personal character: he was 'Father Dan' to everyone in Crowthorne, even after he was 'canonised' in 1970. (Dr. McVerry.)

80. Dr. Kempthorne took this photograph further down the New Wokingham Road, which is technically outside the parish of Crowthorne; but very much part of the village scene. The caption in his album reads: 'Section of 'Middle Bags' brick fields: St. Sebastians.' Maybe 'Middle Bags' was the site of the new 'Pine Ridge' estate. Few people realise that Crowthorne had its own brick works some 200 yards along Oaklands (once Green) Lane. It was owned and operated by William Barker, whose son Cecil still lives in the village. He built his own house, 'Heather Hill', with his own bricks. Sometimes bricks stamped 'Crowthorn' (sic) are found in the area. Surprisingly there were 25 brickworks in the district. (Kempthorne Album.)

81. This part of the village was once the nucleus of Crowthorne. The Post Office was here with its own cancellation stamp: this was only changed from 'Wellington College Station' to 'Crowthorne' in 1928 when the new Post Office opened near the Iron Duke. Barclays Bank had its branch near the station, and only had a small sub-branch in Waterloo Place. This area also was the only one in bounds to Wellington boys, who came down regularly through the Wicket Gate to visit Mr. Bishop's bookshop and other retailers.

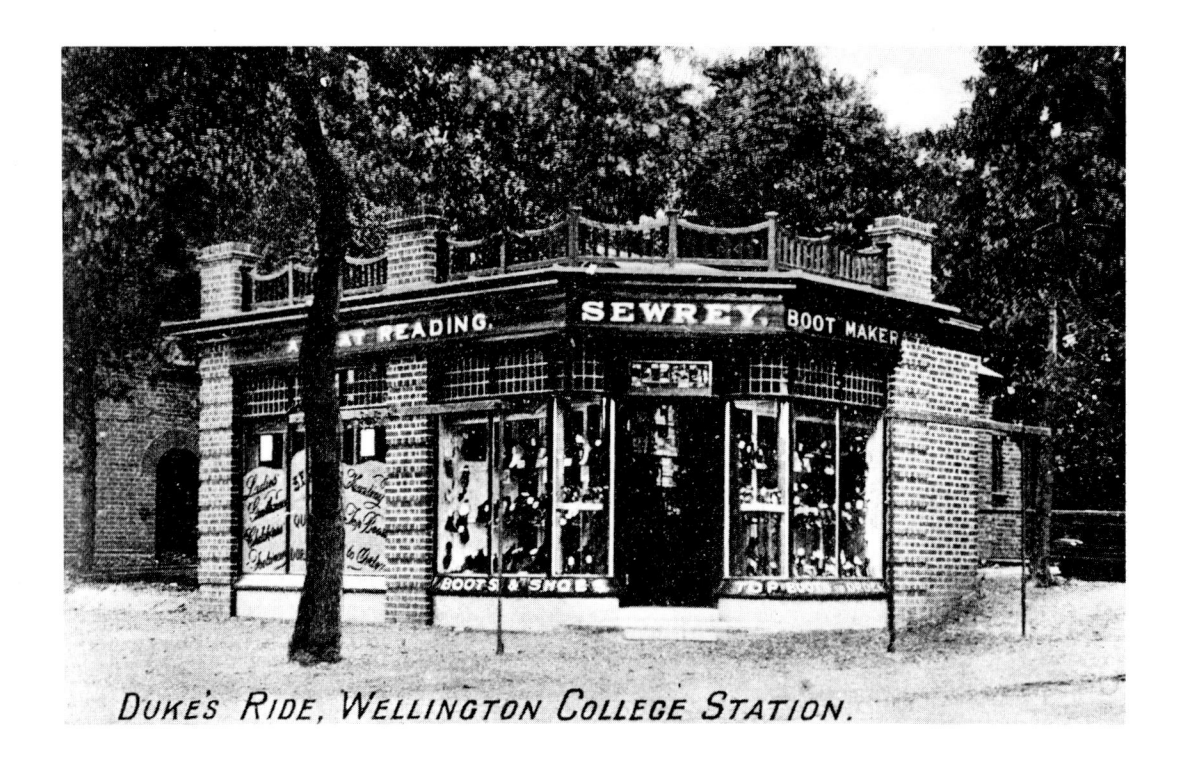

82. Sewrey the bootmaker was really a Reading firm, and made their boots there. The shop lies on Ravenswood Corner down Dukes Ride. Later it was taken over by Hookham the tailor, who did make academic robes for Wellington masters and Oxford dons. Nowadays very few Crowthorne traders actually make anything, or even sell goods. Instead they deal in services, particularly the ever increasing number of estate agents. This shop is now Salon One, the ladies' hair-dresser.

83. This is, of course, the East Berkshire Golf Club. The photograph dates from before 1938, because it was in that year that this club-house was demolished: it is now the site of the car park. Ted Noakes recalls that the Club Secretary at that time was a Capt. Robertson, Scots Greys, said to be the co-founder of the Crowthorne British Legion.

84. Crowthorne Station, which opened for business in 1860, was originally known as 'Wellington College for Crowthorne'. It was only correctly re-named after the Second World War. In those days there were eight staff employed there, as it was a busy station. Now, of course, it is unmanned with no staff at all. Perhaps that may help to explain in a very small way the massive unemployment in modern Britain.

85. The Station Approach between Crowthorne Station and the Wellington Hotel has not changed very much, apart from the bi-coloured brick wall, long since demolished. Of course there were no graffiti on the station walls then.

86. It is sad that this magnificent Wellington Hotel has disappeared virtually without trace. Old Crowthorne residents recall splendid dances and receptions in the noble conservatory. In its long prime the hotel belonged to the Lester Family. After the last war it fell on hard times. One manager in desperation imported a rather seedy strip club, much patronized by Bramshill Police College: one rival publican complained to the authorities, and there was a somewhat chaotic police raid. In the late sixties it became a country club; but it all came to an end, and is only a pleasant memory for old inhabitants.

Wellington College, Barkham Ride.

87. This always used to be known as Barkham Ride as printed, leading as it still does past the Heritage Naturist Club, and on to the village of Barkham; but now has been renamed Heath Ride for some reason. The massive gate marked the southern boundary of the enormous Bearwood estate, and was typical of the gates throughout. The house, which just appears on the edge of the photograph, was originally the gate-keeper's lodge. It was later named South Point. Hedley Bates, who lived there a number of years, remembers the gate as recently as 1958. All the trees in the picture can still be identified. (Hedley Bates.)

WELLINGTONIAN AVENUE
CROWTHORNE

88. So long as it has been there, Wellingtonia Avenue has been a great local attraction, and the subject of great speculation as to its origin and name. The true account seems to have been as follows: in 1853 the Exeter firm of horticulturists, Veitch, sent one of their men named Lobb to collect seeds from the giant conifers discovered in California, and then began to germinate them in quantity. Next year the pre-eminent botanist Sir John Lindley named the tree Wellingtonia in honour of the great Duke, who had died in 1852. Some time later a French botanist decided that it was in fact a Sequoiadendron Giganteum: thank heavens we were spared 'Sequoiadendron Giganteum Avenue'. In 1863 John Walter III, proprietor of the Times and great local benefactor, must have collected a large number of seedlings from Veitch and planted some hundred on the Road to Finchampstead, again in memory of the Duke. Incidentally in its native America the three continues to be called the California Big Tree.

89. The view opposite is from the lower, station end; this looking east from the higher, Ridges end. A recent count of the trees reveals 108. There are only two gaps: a tree struck by lightning long ago; one recently killed by honey fungus. In the 1920s an unbalanced man, who hated anything to do with the Duke of Wellington, climbed thirteen of them and chopped off the tops: the effect can still be seen. In 1985, however, two pupils from Edgbarrow School, Glen Tregoing and Stephen Tarr, volunteered to determine the height of the trees by triangulation. The tallest of the three they measured was 31 46 metres high: 103¼ feet. According to the Guiness Book of Records the tallest Wellingtonia in Britain was 167 feet high; in the world 267 feet in California.

90. This photograph by Dr. Kempthorne is of Heath Pool (or Pond) in 1887. It lies about one third of a mile north of Wellingtonia Avenue and on the Devil's Highway (otherwise the Roman Road at this point). In fact this road forms the northern bank of the pool. There is evidence to suggest that the water table is much lower now than in the past. (Kempthorne Album.)

91. Finchampstead Church is about four miles from the centre of Crowthorne, as the crow flies; but the two parishes are very intimately linked: in fact there is a triangle of Finchampstead, based on the railway line, which stretches one third of a mile into what is generally considered to be Crowthorne village. Finchampstead is many centuries older than its neighbour; a mill there was mentioned in the Domesday Survey. The church was founded in the 12th century; the chancel and nave date from then, as also the bowl of the font. It was added to during the following six centuries. (Kempthorne Album.)

92. Somewhat surprisingly Wokingham town is half a mile closer to Crowthorne than Finchampstead; but the two parishes are separated by Wokingham Without. So it is really cheating to include this photograph by Dr. Kempthorne in 'Crowthorne in old picture postcards'. But this is such a lovely picture of Rose Street that the temptation to include it was too strong. The doctor has really done justice to what is one of the most beautiful frontages in the county or elsewhere. It has been lovingly preserved thanks to the devotion of the people of Wokingham. (Kempthorne Album.)

93. One way back from Wokingham is through St. Sebastians (Wokingham Without). This is not one of Dr. Kempthorne's best photographs; but pictures of old St. Sebastians are hard to come by. It is interesting to have an idea what the hamlet looked like a century ago. It was in fact somewhat earlier in origin than Crowthorne. At the start of the nineteenth century there were 'broom-squires' or 'broom-dashers' dwelling here who made a living from the manufacture of besoms. (Kempthorne Album.)

94. This picture of the 'Who'd-a-tho't it?' has been kindly lent by Morland's brewery. They have calculated by complicated comparisons that the date was 1909. The pub is very old; but nobody seems to know exactly how old. The origin of the peculiar name is fairly obvious: some-one came upon the inn in the middle of the forest, and expressed surprise. But who? One version over from Stratfield Saye. Another attributes it to navvies working on the railway line in the 1840s. But Nurse Gurden, whose step-father Mr. Burn once ran the pub, insists that it was named by visitors to Windsor Castle. (Morland & Co., Abingdon: Mr. H.F. Eveson.)

95. This photograph of St. Sebastians Church was taken a few years after the end of the Second World War. It dates from 1864, and so it was earlier than either of the two Anglican churches in Crowthorne, the temporary one in 1868 and St. John's in 1873. Butterfield was chosen as architect, after the fashionable Blomfield proved too expensive. Blomfield was to design St. John's but Butterfield went on to build Keble College, Oxford, and was later considered the better architect. It seems that the porch was added to the church in the 1920s. (Mr. Peter Randall.)

96. 'Long Thatch' is situated on Honey Hill which is as flat as a pancake! It is an ancient building, at least the single storey part with a chimney at each end. In 1961 the present owner, Mr. Marcus Pym, added a two storey extension, as conformable as possible to the original cottage. Now that this has been re-thatched, the two parts blend together and match remarkably well. (Photograph: Martin Prescott.)

97. Pinewood Hospital, as it was always called in the village, was built early this century as a convalescent hospital for T.B. patients from London. It is now almost forgotten what a dreadful plague tuberculosis was in the 19th century. The treatment was fearsome: if memory serves aright, one lung would be collapsed to enable it to heal. A patient who survived would be sent down to the 'London Open Air Sanatorium' (1911 O.S. map) to enjoy the clean, pine-fresh air at Pinewood. This picture shows the lodge and access gate on Nine Mile Ride. It will be noticed that the board reads: 'M.A.B. PINEWOOD'; this stood for the Metropolitan Asylum Board. (Mick Bell.)

98. Here are the patients' quarters with windows wide open. (Incidentally it is Berks. not Bucks!) Over the years the development of modern drugs, and later mass radiography reduced T.B. to vanishing point; and Pinewood was no longer needed for its original purpose. However, two world wars created new needs: in the first the hospital was used primarily for the treatment of Canadian and other casualties from poison gas; in the second it was occupied by the First New Zealand Hospital, which installed a magnificent operating theatre, left behind when it moved as a farewell present. Thereafter Polish forces moved in. (Mick Bell.)

99. After the Second World War it was wisely decided to convert Pinewood into a local 'Cottage Hospital'; and for some twenty years it filled a real need, like that at Yateley. Then the decision was taken to close it (and Yateley too). It seems the fashionable idea in the sixties was that big is right and small is wrong. Since everyone now has a car – another myth of the sixties (hence Milton Keynes) – it would be sensible for patients to go to Heatherwood or Wexham Park! Crowthorne fought tooth and nail for its precious hospital; but to no avail. For years these fine buildings became a white elephant, offered to all and sundry; but with no takers, except for a proposal to turn it into a sort of hostel for delinquent geriatrics. At long last it became a leisure project, welcome no doubt; but we lament our lost hospital. (Mick Bell.)

100. We have now moved over to the Old Wokingham Road when it was photographed by Dr. Kempthorne in the late 19th century. At first sight it is a little difficult to decide which way we are facing; but the caption clears that up: 'On the upper road to Wokingham. Trees on the left now destroyed.' This suggests that New Wokingham Road had not yet been laid. It also seems likely that the trees had been cut down to make way for the earliest houses on the left of the old road. (Kempthorne Album.)

101. The Observer Corps. The observation post was a short way along the Bracknell Road, up the first rise and on the right of the road. Top row: P.G. Priest, S.W. Sworder, R. Hale, T. Knight, P.G. Blackman, L.M. Leakey. (Head Observer) G.A. Penson, H.C. Smith. Centre row: E.S. Tame, A. Hook, F.T. Angell, G.R. Vaughan, H.M. Ifould, J. Steer, P.C. Rhymer. Seated: H.G. Knee, E. Ankerson, G.B. Davidson, F.W. Bennellick. W.C. Furlong was absent.

102. Windy Ridge(s) is a very old building; but probably not as ancient as Edgbarrow Cottage (plate 54). Some in Crowthorne remember a former owner, a Miss Pledger. She was governess to the five sons and three daughters of Dr. Malim (fifth Master of Wellington: 1921 to 1936). When they all went to school, she decided to establish a tea house at Windy Ridge with a lady friend. This seems to have flourished for a number of years; but in the end she married Dr. Lambert, the school doctor at Wellington; and, one hopes, lived happy ever after. (Photograph: Martin Prescott.)

103. Easthampstead Park is not as old a building as one might suppose. It was built in Elizabethan style about 1860 by the 4th Marquess of Downshire as a family country seat. Yet there was a hunting lodge there centuries before for the king to hunt deer in the Royal Forest of Windsor. In 1531 Katherine of Aragon was in residence when Henry VIII asked her for a divorce. In our own time villagers remember the 6th Marquess, who was something of an eccentric. He used to collect his coal from Bracknell station with a six-in-hand donkey cart. On one occasion he played a trick on his cook, who had displeased him, instead of dismissing her. He moved some of the track of his miniature railway – by night presumably –, next day he persuaded her to come for a spin, and when the train had picked up speed, jumped off, and it ended in the lake. She must have taken the hint, and left. The house is now an educational establishment. (Kempthorne Album.)

104. This picture has long presented a problem as to its date and location. Inspection of the clothes strongly suggests the end of the Edwardian era. It seems most likely that this was Crowthorne celebrating the coronation of King George V in 1911. The locale was clearly a stately home to which the village had been invited. Further examination made it clear that this was South Hill Park, originally built in 1760. After changing hands many times it was bought by Sir William Hayter in 1853. Twenty-five years later he was found drowned presumably in the fish pond. His son Sir Arthur rebuilt most of the mansion towards the end of the 19th century. He became Lord Haversham in 1906. So he would appear to have played the host to Crowthorne. (John Drew.)

105. This is Linda Cottage, the oldest building in Owlsmoor, which used to be part of the ecclesiastical and secular parish of Crowthorne. It was built in 1882 by a Mr. New – which was surely not why the hamlet was originally called 'New-found-out': if so what had he done? The well is genuine. The object on the chimney-stack is a fire-mark (see inset) which was supplied by the insurance company to show that you had paid your premium. They would only send their fire-engine to fight your fire if it was in place. Otherwise you could go to blazes!

106. The old 'Bull and Butcher' in College Town, photographed here in 1905, was pulled down and rebuilt in 1938. It is said that in the old bar a man could touch the floor and ceiling with his finger-tips simultaneously. Herbert Hale has a nice story about his mother and the pub. It seems she used to go round with her father, Mr. Elphick, in the mid-1890s when he toured College Town collecting insurance money. He always went into this pub for a plowman's lunch and two penn'orth of ale. One day he was ill and sent her out on her own, aged about twelve. She decided to go into the Bull and Butcher and have beer with her lunch. She thought is was expected of her; though she hated it.

107. When the Chapel of Christ the King at the Royal Military College Sandhurst was originally built, the sanctuary and altar, as shown, faced towards the south and the old building, instead of to the traditional east. After the end of the First World War it was decided to extend it, and the opportunity was taken to construct a new chancel and nave at right angles to the original structure, so that now the altar is at the east end. The old sanctuary became the South African Memorial Chapel. This arrangement prompts the question why Christian churches are orientated to the east. Various reasons have been mooted; but the best authorities make it clear that it is because the sun rises in the east, a purely pagan idea. (Mick Bell.)

108. This volume ends with a last picture from Dr. Kempthorne's album, and a final conundrum. Where is this church? The local newspaper, the Wokingham (Crowthorne) Times, printed the picture in the hope that a reader would identify it; but to no avail. Yet all Dr. Kempthorne's photographs were of local views (except for Taunton, where the family spent their summer holidays). Still there is one slight clue. The good doctor always seemed to fill his album in sequence as he took his pictures. Here the previous page included a shot of a Thames tow-path, while the next one featured Thames river scenes round Eton and Windsor. So perhaps this church, if it still exists, is in that area. It will be interesting to find out. (Kempthorne Album.)